Owls
Coloring Book

Noelle Dahlen

DOVER PUBLICATIONS, INC.
Mineola, New York

This whimsical coloring collection features thirty adorable owl designs to color—playing with animal friends, sleeping under an umbrella in the rain, attending school, and more imaginative scenes. Detailed designs are perfect for the enthusiastic colorist, and the perforated pages make displaying finished work easy!

Copyright

Copyright © 2013, 2015 by Dover Publications, Inc.
All rights reserved.

Bibliographical Note

Owls Coloring Book, first published by Dover Publications, Inc., in 2015, is a revised edition of the work originally published by Dover in 2013.

International Standard Book Number

ISBN-13: 978-0-486-80211-4
ISBN-10: 0-486-80211-6

Manufactured in the United States by LSC Communications
80211609   2016
www.doverpublications.com

Draw Your Own Owls Design